UNIQUE ORIGAMI

A Comprehensive Guide with Exceptional Concept to Folding Star Paper Strips with Over 600 Sheets for Easy Arts Paper Craft Gift for Origami Lucky Stars

Kristen Anderson

TABLE OF CONTENT

INTRODUCTION 3

CHAPTER 1 7

TYPES OF ORIGAMI 7

CHAPTER 2 23

WHAT TO KNOW ABOUT STAR ORIGAMI? 23

CHAPTER 3 33

HOW TO CREATE STAR ORIGAMI 33

CHAPTER 4 40

IMPORTANCE OF CREATING ORIGAMI 40

CHAPTER 5 45

CONCLUSION 45

INTRODUCTION

Origami stars are charming and delightful creations that upload a hint of elegance to any setting. Originating from the historical Japanese artwork of paper folding, origami stars are normally made from small, square pieces of paper and can variety in complexity from easy designs appropriate for beginners to difficult styles requiring superior folding competencies.

The art of origami itself has a rich history, relationship returned to historic Japan in which it changed into to start with used for ceremonial and religious purposes. over the years, it has advanced into a beloved and extensively practiced form of creative expression worldwide. Origami stars, particularly, have gained recognition for their versatility and symbolic significance.

Crafting an origami megastar frequently involves unique folds and smart manipulations of the paper to create a 3-dimensional shape. The cease end result is a fascinating superstar shape that can be used for numerous decorative functions. whether or not placing from a string to create a festive garland, redecorating gift programs, or actually scattered as table decor, origami stars bring a hint of hand-crafted beauty to any event.

Origami stars come in various designs, consisting of the traditional

5-pointed celebrity or extra problematic modular stars made with the aid of combining a couple of folded devices. additionally, they may be made from extraordinary colors and styles of paper, bearing in mind limitless innovative opportunities.

Aside from their aesthetic appeal, origami stars can bring personal which means and importance. They make thoughtful items, because the time and effort put into developing them reveal care and attention to element. additionally, the act of folding the paper may be a meditative and enjoyable experience, making origami stars no longer most effective visually beautiful but also a healing and enjoyable craft.

whether or not you are a pro origami enthusiast or a novice seeking out a innovative outlet, origami stars provide a satisfying adventure into the sector of paper folding. With a few sheets of paper and a chunk of patience, you can rework easy materials into beautiful, hand-crafted stars that shine with artistic expression.

CHAPTER 1

TYPES OF ORIGAMI

conventional Origami:

This involves folding paper into primary shapes and figures, which includes animals, flora, and geometric forms. conventional origami frequently follows traditional designs and techniques handed down thru generations.

Modular Origami:

Modular origami includes developing complex systems by interlocking multiple folded units. these gadgets are normally easy shapes like triangles, squares, or rectangles, that are then blended to form large and greater difficult designs.

Wet-Folding Origami:

In moist-folding, artists dampen the paper earlier than folding it. This method permits for more rounded and sculptural shapes, developing a softer and greater organic appearance inside the final piece.

Kirigami:

whilst now not strictly origami, kirigami combines folding with cutting. Artists make precise cuts in the paper similarly to folding, resulting in three-dimensional pop-up systems or complex designs.

Motion Origami:

also called kinetic origami, motion origami involves developing models which could circulate or alternate form. these designs frequently comprise folds that permit the finished piece to carry out a specific action, which includes flapping wings or commencing and final.

Tessellation Origami:

Tessellation origami is characterized by means of repeating geometric patterns across the entire floor of the paper. Artists use unique folding techniques to create complex and visually beautiful tessellated designs.

3D Origami:

In three-D origami, artists create sculptures using a couple of folded paper modules, generally small triangular pieces, to build up a three-dimensional structure. This method is famous for creating big and colorful sculptures.

Cash Origami:

money origami includes folding banknotes into numerous shapes and designs. It provides an element of creativity to foreign money, turning payments into miniature works of art.

Origami architecture:

Origami architecture entails developing complicated paper systems that resemble homes and architectural bureaucracy. those designs regularly comprise more than one layers of paper to add intensity and element.

Mathematical Origami:

This type of origami explores mathematical concepts and standards thru folding. Mathematicians and educators regularly use origami to educate geometry, symmetry, and other mathematical ideas.

whilst these classes embody a large variety of origami patterns, many artists revel in combining techniques and growing their very own precise variations. The functions of origami can range from decorative and creative expression to educational functions, such as coaching geometry, spatial relationships, and trouble-fixing talents.

Origami Tessellations:

Tessellation origami is a fascinating subset where artists create problematic styles by repeating a single folded form throughout the complete sheet of paper. The ensuing designs can be highly specific and visually lovely, showcasing the mathematical and geometric factors of origami.

Kusudama Origami:

Kusudama is a sort of modular origami wherein a couple of units are assembled to create a spherical form. these origami balls are regularly used as decorations or embellishes, and they arrive in various sizes and complexities.

Origami in technological know-how and generation:

Origami standards have inspired improvements in technology and engineering. Scientists and engineers have explored the usage of origami folding techniques to layout structures, medical devices, or even spacecraft additives. The ability to fold and spread efficiently is valuable in creating compact and deployable structures.

Pop-Up Origami:

Pop-up origami involves growing three-dimensional structures that "pop up" whilst the paper is opened. This type of origami is frequently utilized in making greeting playing cards, storybooks, and different paper crafts in which wonder and dimensionality are desired.

Environmental Origami:

A few origami recognitions on using recycled or green materials to create their folded masterpieces. Environmental origami explores sustainability and encourages the use of paper alternatives or repurposed substances.

Origami remedy:

Origami is every now and then used as a healing device to reduce strain and sell mindfulness. The repetitive and targeted nature of folding will have a chilled impact, making origami a famous interest in pressure comfort and intellectual fitness programs.

Origami fashion:

Designers have included origami strategies into fashion, developing clothes and accessories with folded elements. Origami fashion often explores the intersection of way of life and modernity, showcasing the versatility of paper as a material.

Origami and education:

Origami is extensively used as an academic tool to train diverse subjects, along with mathematics, geometry, and cultural studies. It facilitates students develop spatial reasoning competencies, endurance, and a deeper understanding of abstract standards through hands-on folding.

Origami as performance art:

a few artists take origami past static creations and carry out stay origami demonstrations. those performances may additionally contain creating large-scale portions, participating with different artists, or combining origami with different artwork forms like dance or music.

Collaborative Origami tasks:

The origami network regularly engages in collaborative initiatives in which a couple of artists make contributions folded pieces to create massive and intricate displays. those tasks show off the variety and creativity inside the origami community.

Origami maintains to adapt and adapt to new contexts, with artists pushing the limits of what may be accomplished with the easy act of folding paper. The art shape's interdisciplinary nature permits it to intersect with various fields, making it a versatile and constantly inspiring exercise.

Origami has deep connections to mathematical ideas, inclusive of geometry, symmetry, and topology. Mathematicians observe origami to recognize folding algorithms and discover mathematical theorems, making it a captivating intersection of art and math.

Origami and Robotics:

The standards of origami folding have motivated the field of robotics. Engineers and researchers have advanced robots with folding and unfolding abilities inspired through origami, permitting compact and adaptable robotic structures.

Origami and area Exploration:

Origami principles had been taken into consideration for area exploration missions. Folding systems may be superb for spacecraft additives, as they allow for compact garage throughout launch and efficient deployment in area.

Origami-inspired substances:

Scientists and engineers have explored creating materials stimulated by using origami folds. those materials can have packages in creating light-weight and flexible structures, from medical gadgets to structure.

Origami and Cultural Celebrations:

Many cultures comprise origami into their conventional celebrations. In Japan, as an instance, origami cranes are regularly folded and given as symbols of peace and well-wishing at some point of weddings and other festive occasions.

Origami in marketing and layout:

Origami is on occasion utilized in marketing campaigns and product design. agencies leverage the visible attraction and symbolism of origami to create memorable and aesthetically beautiful promotional substances.

Origami in therapy and Rehabilitation:

beyond strain comfort, origami has determined programs in healing settings for individuals recovering from bodily injuries or present process rehabilitation. the proper movements required in folding can useful resource in first-class motor talent improvement.

Origami Conventions and Exhibitions:

The origami community gathers at conventions and exhibitions international to share strategies, showcase creations, and collaborate on tasks. those activities provide a platform for enthusiasts to attach, analyze, and have fun the artwork shape.

Origami and Augmented truth:

some artists and architects have explored combining origami with augmented truth (AR) generation. This integration lets in visitors to revel in both the bodily origami piece and additional virtual factors, enhancing the interactive nature of the artwork.

Origami as Cultural historical past:

Origami is an imperative part of eastern cultural heritage, and its significance extends past creative expression. it is often associated with mindfulness, persistence, and the appreciation of simplicity and beauty in ordinary life.

Origami's have an impact on maintains to expand into numerous fields, from science and era to art and training. As artists and innovators discover new opportunities, the artwork of folding paper remains a dynamic and evolving exercise with a wealthy history and promising destiny.

CHAPTER 2

WHAT TO KNOW ABOUT STAR ORIGAMI?

problem ranges: superstar origami can range from simple designs appropriate for novices to extra complicated ones that require advanced folding strategies. start with simple models and gradually development to greater complicated ones as you advantage revel in.

Paper desire: the choice of paper is critical in origami. Thinner papers are typically less complicated to fold; however, they may now not maintain their shape as properly. experiment with different sorts of paper to discover what works pleasant for the unique star layout you're attempting.

Diagrams or Tutorials: look for origami diagrams or video tutorials that manual you through the folding technique. Many origami artists and websites provide step-via-step commands, which may be very useful, mainly for complicated designs.

Precision subjects: Accuracy in folding is vital for attaining a neat and well-defined megastar form. take note of info like crease lines and alignment to ensure your origami celebrity seems as supposed.

exercise and staying power: Origami, like any artwork form, calls for exercise. don't be discouraged in case your first attempts don't flip out perfectly. keep training, and you will enhance your folding capabilities over the years.

traditional Five-Pointed famous person:

this is one of the most not unusual origami stars and is regularly associated with the traditional folded paper stars. It normally entails folding a square sheet of paper into a modular layout to create 5 factors.

Fortunate big name (Shuriken):

fortunate stars, additionally referred to as origami shuriken, are small, colorful paper stars which are frequently made with lengthy, thin strips of paper. they may be typically folded from strips of paper with diverse shades and styles and are considered symbols of good fortune.

Moravian star:

The Moravian megastar is a 3-dimensional star with a unique geometric layout. it's far regularly crafted from more than one portions of paper or modules that are assembled to shape a complicated, multi-pointed big name. Moravian stars are used for ornamental purposes, specifically for the duration of the vacation season.

Twisted Paper celebrity:

This sort of origami famous person involves twisting paper strips to create a visually interesting and dynamic superstar form. it is able to be a piece extra complex than traditional flat stars and frequently requires cautious manipulation of the paper.

3D Modular Stars:

some origami stars are made by using assembling multiple modular devices. those units are folded one by one after which mixed to shape a 3-dimensional star. The Sonobe unit is a famous example used in creating modular stars.

Hoshi (Pointed) Stars:

Hoshi stars are folded from a rectangular sheet of paper and feature multiple factors radiating outward. they could have varying numbers of factors, and the folding method may additionally fluctuate primarily based on the desired outcome.

Cultural importance: Origami stars have cultural importance in various societies around the world. In Japan, as an instance, origami has deep-rooted cultural significance, and stars made via origami can be related to Shinto traditions, fairs, or used as decorations. lucky stars, or origami shuriken, have a unique place in Japanese tradition, symbolizing proper good fortune, safety, and sometimes even keeping off evil spirits. In different cultures, stars are probably used as spiritual symbols or as decorations all through festive activities.

Advanced Folding techniques: As your development to your origami adventure, you can stumble upon extra superior folding strategies required for intricate megastar designs. Modular origami is a technique wherein multiple devices are folded and then assembled to create a complicated shape. Stars just like the Moravian big name frequently involve modular folding. The Sonobe unit is a essential modular origami unit utilized in growing 3-dimensional stars. This approach calls for precision in folding every unit and endurance in assembling them to acquire the very last big name shape.

moreover, some stars involve twists and turns in the paper to create visually hanging effects. Twisted paper stars, for example, require careful manipulation of paper strips to attain an attractive and dynamic megastar form. those advanced techniques task origami enthusiasts to hone their capabilities, selling creativity and attention to element.

versions in Origami Stars: Origami stars are available in numerous shapes, sizes, and designs, allowing for a huge variety of creative expression. even as the traditional 5-pointed star is a conventional design, there are stars with one of a kind numbers of points, ranging from 4 to 12 or extra. each version may require particular folding sequences and strategies.

The Moravian superstar, originating from the Moravian Church, is an elaborate geometric layout with more than one factors. Its assembly entails precision in connecting the modules to shape the final 3-dimensional megastar. Moravian stars are regularly associated with Christmas decorations and have come to be popular beyond their cultural origins.

Fortunate stars, or origami shuriken, are smaller, frequently made from thin strips of paper, and may be folded speedy once you grasp the technique. they may be typically used in crafting colorful garlands, mobiles, or honestly as tokens of good success.

Experimenting with extraordinary paper sorts, textures, and patterns provides some other layer of variant to origami stars. From conventional simple origami paper to textured or patterned craft paper, the selection of cloth can drastically effect the final look of the megastar.

academic and therapeutic benefits: beyond their aesthetic attraction, origami stars provide academic and healing blessings. Folding origami enhances spatial reasoning, first-rate motor skills, and awareness. it is regularly used as an academic device to train geometry and mathematical concepts. additionally, origami will have healing effects, selling mindfulness and relaxation as individual's cognizance on the appropriate actions required within the folding manner.

In end, origami stars represent a various and culturally rich issue of the wider origami lifestyle. whether you are attracted to the simplicity of lucky stars or the complexity of modular and twisted designs, exploring the arena of origami stars can be a profitable and innovative adventure.

CHAPTER 3

HOW TO CREATE STAR ORIGAMI

Materials wanted:

Square Paper:

Origami stars are typically crafted from square sheets of paper. you may use origami paper, that is mainly designed for origami and comes in various shades and styles. if you don't have origami paper, you may cut a rectangular from everyday paper.

Scissors (non-obligatory):

in case you're now not the use of pre-reduce origami paper and want to make a square from everyday paper, you may need scissors to reduce it into a rectangular form.

Folding floor:

pick out a clean and flat floor to fold your origami. this will be a desk, table, or every other stable floor.

Patience and Precision:

Origami requires patience and precision. Take your time and observe the commands cautiously to reap the desired end result.

Step 1: choose Your Paper: begin by choosing a rectangular piece of origami paper. if you don't have origami paper, you could reduce a rectangular from ordinary paper. make sure that the paper is colorful and not too thick for less difficult folding.

Step 2: begin with a Diagonal Fold: region your square paper on a flat floor with the color side facing down. Fold it in half of diagonally, bringing one corner to meet the alternative nook. ensure the edges align perfectly and make a sharp crease. unfold the paper to reveal a crease walking from one corner to some other.

Step 3: Diagonal Fold in the different direction: Fold the paper in half of again, this time bringing one corner to satisfy the alternative nook along the opposite diagonal. make certain the edges align perfectly, and make a sharp crease. unfold the paper again to reveal a go-formed crease pattern.

Step 4: Fold the edges to the middle: Take every nook of the square and fold it towards the center, the use of the intersecting creases as a guide. You need to become with a smaller rectangular.

Step 5: Repeat the previous Step: turn the paper over and repeat the process on the alternative aspect. Fold every corner toward the center, creating a smaller rectangular.

Step 6: Fold the Corners to the center once more: Now, take each of the newly shaped corners and fold them closer to the center of the rectangular. You ought to grow to be with an excellent smaller square.

Step 7: Create the preliminary Base: spread the corners you simply folded inside the preceding step. you will be aware that there are current creases out of yours in advance folds. Push the perimeters of the square inwards along those creases, collapsing the paper into an initial base.

Step 8: form a Water Bomb Base: Fold the pinnacle and bottom edges of the initial base towards the middle, forming a rectangle. Now, fold the left and proper edges closer to the middle as properly. This have to result in a smaller rectangular with flaps on each facet.

Step 9: Fold the Flaps: Take one of the flaps and fold it in the direction of the middle. Repeat this on the alternative three flaps, creating a smaller rectangular again.

Step 10: Create the Diamond shape: preserve the paper in order that the open flaps are at the bottom. Take the top layer of the proper flap and fold it toward the middle. Repeat this at the left facet as well. you may grow to be with a diamond shape.

Step 11: Fold the top Flap: Fold the pinnacle flap of the diamond down closer to the lowest, aligning it with the lowest part. this could create a triangular form.

Step 12: Fold the facet Flaps: Fold the left and proper flaps towards the center, forming a smaller triangle. these flaps will become the palms of your famous person.

Step 13: Repeat on the other facet: turn the paper over and repeat steps eleven and 12 on the opposite aspect.

Step 14: end the megastar: gently unfold the flaps on both facets, revealing the finished origami famous person. adjust the angles of the flaps to provide your celebrity its very last form.

CHAPTER 4

IMPORTANCE OF CREATING ORIGAMI

Origami, the historic Japanese art of paper folding, is not merely a activity or a creative outlet; it holds profound significance that transcends its aesthetic appeal. The significance of making origami extends beyond the realms of entertainment and inventive expression, encompassing cognitive, cultural, educational, and healing dimensions.

At its core, origami is a mental workout that engages the mind in a unique manner. The complex folds and specific maneuvers required to convert a flat sheet of paper right into a 3-dimensional masterpiece stimulate cognitive features along with spatial focus, trouble-solving, and fine motor talents. This intellectual dexterity is in particular useful for individuals of all ages, from children growing critical cognitive skills to seniors keeping mental acuity.

Origami serves as a tangible manifestation of cultural historical past and way of life. Rooted in eastern lifestyle, it has deep ancient roots, with its origins dating again to the 6th century. The art form encapsulates the concepts of staying power, precision, and ease, reflecting traditional jap aesthetics. via the introduction of origami, people can connect with and recognize the wealthy cultural tapestry from which it emerges, fostering cross-cultural expertise and appreciation.

From an academic angle, origami serves as a revolutionary teaching device across diverse disciplines. In arithmetic, it introduces ideas like symmetry, geometry, and share, making summary concepts greater on hand and tangible. In technological know-how, origami models can illustrate ideas of physics, engineering, and anatomy, offering a arms-on approach to studying complicated topics. furthermore, origami has been included into language arts, teaching persistence, concentration, and the significance of following commands.

The therapeutic blessings of origami are gaining recognition in fields such as psychology and occupational therapy. engaging inside the repetitive and rhythmic technique of folding paper may have a relaxing effect, reducing stress and tension. the point of interest required for difficult folding promotes mindfulness, allowing individuals to be present in the second and cultivate a experience of tranquility. In healing settings, origami has been utilized as a tool for self-expression, conversation, and rehabilitation, imparting a non-verbal outlet for feelings and creativity.

Origami's environmental impact also adds to its significance in the current context. unlike many artwork bureaucracies that require sizeable resources and convey waste, origami relies completely on a sheet of paper. The sustainability and minimum ecological footprint of origami align with present day issues about environmental conservation and responsible consumption. by way of selling an art shape that makes use of a conveniently to be had and recyclable fabric, people can make contributions to a eco-friendlier method to creativity.

moreover, origami fosters a experience of accomplishment and self-esteem. As individuals master more and more complicated folding patterns, they experience a tangible progression in their abilities, boosting self-assurance and perseverance. This experience of success is mainly valuable for kids, instilling a wonderful mind-set closer to gaining knowledge of and hassle-fixing which could enlarge into different areas of their lives.

CHAPTER 5
CONCLUSION

Creating origami stars may be a lovely and rewarding creative enterprise. whether or not you are a amateur or an experienced origami fanatic, folding paper into problematic star shapes lets in you to explore creativity, persistence, and precision. The procedure of transforming a flat sheet of paper right into a 3-dimensional famous person can be both meditative and hard, promoting attention and first-rate motor competencies.

Origami stars come in various designs, starting from easy to complicated, providing a huge range of options for artists of all skill stages. The delight of completing a star fold and witnessing the transformation of a humble piece of paper into a lovely geometric creation is a unique and pleasurable enjoy.

Beyond the cultured appeal, origami stars also maintain cultural significance in exceptional traditions. for instance, they may be frequently related to celebrations, decorations, and symbolism. Many humans use origami stars as embellishes all through festive occasions or as thoughtful presents. the versatility of these creations lets in for customization and edition to various themes and occasions.

In end, superstar origami isn't always only a craft but an artwork form that combines way of life, creativity, and mindfulness. the adventure of folding paper stars can carry pleasure, relaxation, and a feel of achievement. whether or not pursued as a interest, a shape of self-expression, or a cultural exercise, creating origami stars is a lovely and significant activity for individuals of every age.

Printed in Great Britain
by Amazon